W9-AEE-048

I LIKE SPORTS STARS!

Read About
Carmelo
Anthony

David P. Torsiello

Enslow Elementary
an imprint of
Enslow Publishers, Inc.
40 Industrial Road
Box 398
Berkeley Heights, NJ 07922
USA
http://www.enslow.com

South Huntington Pub. Lib.
145 Pidgeon Hill Rd.
Huntington Sta., N.Y. 11746

For my cousin Tom Sorrentino. Hope he brings home the trophy for you, cuz.

CONTENTS

WORDS TO KNOW

defense—Keeping the other team from scoring.

dribble—When you bounce the ball off the floor with your fingertips.

playoffs—A series of games played to determine a champion.

rebound—Grabbing the ball after a missed shot.

small forward—One of the positions on a basketball team.

steal—When you take the ball away from another player.

Carmelo Anthony was born on May 29, 1984. He plays basketball for the New York Knicks.

Carmelo was born in Brooklyn and grew up in Baltimore. After high school, he went to Syracuse University.

n his first year of college,
Carmelo led his team to
the title!

Carmelo joined the
Denver Nuggets in
2003. He proved he
was a great player
right away.

Carmelo's position is small forward. He can take the ball and dribble close to the basket. Or he can shoot the ball from far away.

Carmelo also has to
play defense.
If he plays it well, he
might steal the ball!

Carmelo must also rebound. This is when you grab the ball after a missed shot.

In 2008, Carmelo played for
Team USA in the Olympics.
The team won the gold medal
that year!

Carmelo was traded to the Knicks in 2011. In his third game with the team, they played the Miami Heat. Carmelo played against LeBron James. The Knicks won!

Carmelo wants to win
just one more thing . . .
a championship with the
Knicks!

Further Reading

Anthony, Carmelo, and Greg Brown. *Carmelo Anthony: It's Just The Beginning.* Kirkland, Wash.: Positively for Kids, 2004.

Ladewski, Paul. *Megastars 2010.* New York: Scholastic, 2010.

Internet Address

NBA.com—Carmelo Anthony

http://www.nba.com/playerfile/carmelo_anthony/

   INDEX